Contents

What is paper? 4

What happens when you throw
   paper away? 6

What is recycling? 8

How can I reuse old paper? 10

What can I make with paper cups
   and bags? 14

What else can I make with paper? 16

Make your own magazine nameplate 18

Recycling quiz 22

Glossary .23

Find out more 24

Index 24

Some words are shown in bold, **like this**. You can find them in the glossary on page 23.

What is paper?

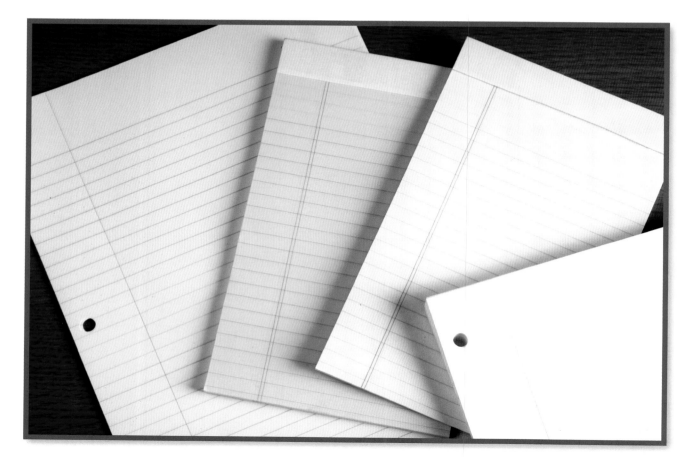

Paper is a **material** we write on.

Paper is made from trees.

Books, magazines, newspapers, and notepads are all made of paper.

Napkins, plates, and cups can all be made of paper, too!

What happens when you throw paper away?

Paper is very useful.

But when you have finished with it, do you throw it away?

If you throw paper away it will end up at a rubbish tip.

It will be buried in the ground and may stay there for a very long time.

What is recycling?

It is much better to **recycle** paper instead of throwing it away.

Separate paper from your other rubbish and then put it in a recycling bin.

The paper will be collected and taken to a **factory**.

Then the paper will be made into something new.

How can I reuse old paper?

You can also use old paper to make your own new things.

When you have finished with something made out of paper, put it to one side instead of throwing it away.

Soon you will have lots of paper waiting to be reused.

You are ready to turn your rubbish into riches!

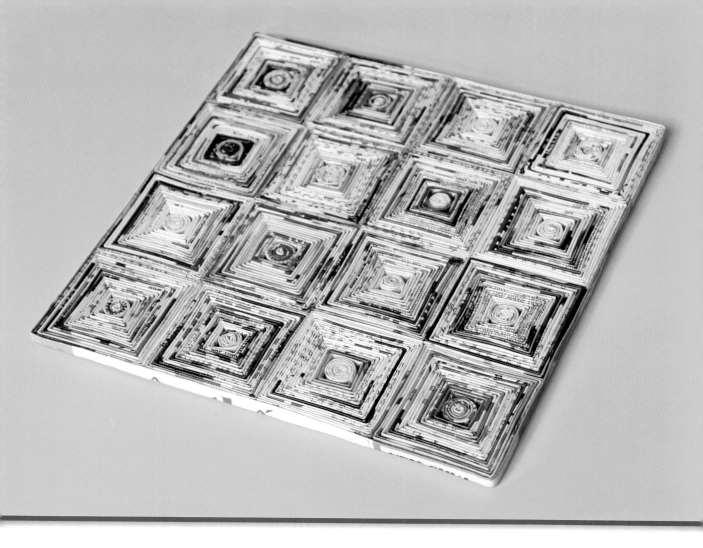

Magazines can be made into colourful table mats.

This table mat has been made by folding up pages from magazines.

You can also cut up paper to make beautiful **mosaics**.

This picture of a bird is made out of lots of tiny pieces of old paper.

What can I make with paper cups and bags?

You can use an old paper cup to make a fun ball-and-cup game.

Try to catch the ball in the cup – it's harder than it looks!

Paper bags make great puppets!

What sort of paper bag puppet will you make?

What else can I make with paper?

You can make all sorts of things with **papier mâché**.

These children are wearing papier mâché masks.

Making papier mâché can be a bit messy.

Why not keep clean by wearing an apron made of old newspapers?

Make your own magazine nameplate

You can use old magazines to make a nameplate for your bedroom door.

You will need a piece of card, scissors, glue, and a pile of old magazines.

First, decide what you want your nameplate to say.

Then cut out the letters that you need from the magazines. Do not use sharp scissors without help from an adult.

Arrange the letters in the right order on the card.

Then carefully glue each letter to the card.

Wait for the glue to dry.

Your nameplate is ready to be fixed
to your bedroom door!

Recycling quiz

One of these things is made from **recycled** paper. Can you guess which one? (Answer on page 24.)

Glossary

 **factory** building where something is made

 **material** what something is made of

 **mosaic** picture made from small pieces of paper, glass, or tiles

 **papier mâché** mixture of shredded paper and glue used to make things. It goes hard when it is dry.

 **recycle** break down a material and use it again to make something new

Find out more

Ask an adult to help you make fun things with paper using the websites below.

Ball-and-cup game: **www.lakeshorelearning. com/general_content/free_resources/crafts/mt_ catchthebead.jsp**

Fruit and vegetables: **familyfun.go.com/crafts/papier-mache-veggies-661990/**

Table mats: **www.clevernesting.com/2009/07/ recycled-magazine-page-coaster-tutorial/**

Answer to question on page 22
The cat is made from recycled paper.

Index

factories 9, 23

magazines 5, 12, 18–21

masks 16

materials 4, 23

mosaics 13, 23

nameplate 18–21

papier mâché 16, 17, 23

puppets 15

recycling 8, 9, 22, 23

rubbish tip 7